Fun Facts & Trivia
1951 - A Year In Review

ISBN: 9798568278504

INDEX

FIRST EDITION

1951

January
M	T	W	T	F	S	S
1	2	3	4	5	6	7
8	9	10	11	12	13	14
15	16	17	18	19	20	21
22	23	24	25	26	27	28
29	30	31				

◐:1 ●:7 ◑:15 ○:23 ◐:30

February
M	T	W	T	F	S	S
			1	2	3	4
5	6	7	8	9	10	11
12	13	14	15	16	17	18
19	20	21	22	23	24	25
26	27	28				

●:6 ◑:13 ○:21 ◐:28

March
M	T	W	T	F	S	S
			1	2	3	4
5	6	7	8	9	10	11
12	13	14	15	16	17	18
19	20	21	22	23	24	25
26	27	28	29	30	31	

●:7 ◑:15 ○:23 ◐:30

April
M	T	W	T	F	S	S
						1
2	3	4	5	6	7	8
9	10	11	12	13	14	15
16	17	18	19	20	21	22
23	24	25	26	27	28	29
30						

●:6 ◑:14 ○:21 ◐:28

May
M	T	W	T	F	S	S
	1	2	3	4	5	6
7	8	9	10	11	12	13
14	15	16	17	18	19	20
21	22	23	24	25	26	27
28	29	30	31			

●:6 ◑:14 ○:21 ◐:27

June
M	T	W	T	F	S	S
				1	2	3
4	5	6	7	8	9	10
11	12	13	14	15	16	17
18	19	20	21	22	23	24
25	26	27	28	29	30	

●:4 ◑:12 ○:19 ◐:26

July
M	T	W	T	F	S	S
						1
2	3	4	5	6	7	8
9	10	11	12	13	14	15
16	17	18	19	20	21	22
23	24	25	26	27	28	29
30	31					

●:4 ◑:12 ○:18 ◐:25

August
M	T	W	T	F	S	S
		1	2	3	4	5
6	7	8	9	10	11	12
13	14	15	16	17	18	19
20	21	22	23	24	25	26
27	28	29	30	31		

●:2 ◑:10 ○:17 ◐:24

September
M	T	W	T	F	S	S
					1	2
3	4	5	6	7	8	9
10	11	12	13	14	15	16
17	18	19	20	21	22	23
24	25	26	27	28	29	30

●:1 ◑:8 ○:15 ◐:23

October
M	T	W	T	F	S	S
1	2	3	4	5	6	7
8	9	10	11	12	13	14
15	16	17	18	19	20	21
22	23	24	25	26	27	28
29	30	31				

●:1 ◑:8 ○:15 ◐:22 ●:30

November
M	T	W	T	F	S	S
			1	2	3	4
5	6	7	8	9	10	11
12	13	14	15	16	17	18
19	20	21	22	23	24	25
26	27	28	29	30		

◑:6 ○:13 ◐:21 ●:29

December
M	T	W	T	F	S	S
					1	2
3	4	5	6	7	8	9
10	11	12	13	14	15	16
17	18	19	20	21	22	23
24	25	26	27	28	29	30
31						

◑:5 ○:13 ◐:21 ●:28

PEOPLE IN HIGH OFFICE

Monarch - King George VI
Reign: 11th December 1936 - 6th February 1952
Predecessor: Edward VIII
Successor: Elizabeth II

United Kingdom

Prime Minister
Clement Attlee
Labour Party
26th July 1945 - 26th October 1951

Prime Minister
Winston Churchill
Conservative Party
26th October 1951 - 5th April 1955

Canada

Australia

United States

Prime Minister
Sir Robert Menzies
Liberal (Coalition)
19th December 1949
- 26th January 1966

Prime Minister
Louis St. Laurent
Liberal Party
15th November 1948
- 21st June 1957

President
Harry S. Truman
Democratic Party
12th April 1945
- 20th January 1953

Brazil	**President** Eurico Gaspar Dutra (1946-1951) Getúlio Vargas (1951-1954)
China	**Premier** Chen Cheng (1950-1954)
Cuba	**President** Carlos Prío Socarrás (1948-1952)
France	**President** Vincent Auriol (1947-1954)
India	**Prime Minister** Jawaharlal Nehru (1947-1964)
Ireland	**Taoiseach of Ireland** John A. Costello (1948-1951) Éamon de Valera (1951-1954)
Italy	**Prime Minister** Alcide De Gasperi (1945-1953)
Japan	**Prime Minister** Shigeru Yoshida (1948-1954)

Mexico	President Miguel Alemán Valdés (1946-1952)
New Zealand	Prime Minister Sidney Holland (1949-1957)
Pakistan	Prime Minister Liaquat Ali Khan (1947-1951) Khawaja Nazimuddin (1951-1953)
Spain	President Francisco Franco (1938-1973)
South Africa	Prime Minister Daniel François Malan (1948-1954)
Soviet Union	Communist Party Leader Joseph Stalin (1922-1953)
Turkey	Prime Minister Adnan Menderes (1950-1960)
West Germany	Chancellor Konrad Adenauer (1949-1963)

BRITISH NEWS & EVENTS

JAN

The British Board of Film Censors introduces an X rating (classed as "extremely graphic" and suitable for those aged 16 and over) as a result of the Wheare Report on censorship.

The Ford Consul, unveiled at the London Motor Show in October 1950, goes on sale in the United Kingdom.

1st The first episode of radio soap opera The Archers is broadcast nationally on the BBC Light Programme. *Interesting facts: Today, having aired over 19,100 episodes, it is the world's longest-running drama. With over five million listeners it is also Radio 4's most listened-to non-news programme and holds the record for BBC Radio online listening figures.*

9th The government announces the abandonment of the Tanganyika groundnut scheme to cultivate tracts of Tanganyika (modern-day Tanzania) with peanuts. *Note: Launched in the aftermath of World War II by the administration of Prime Minister Clement Attlee, the project (which cost of £36,500,000), was popularly seen as a symbol of government failure in late colonial Africa.*

FEB

The Ferranti Mark 1, the world's first commercially available general-purpose electronic computer, is delivered to the University of Manchester.

21st February: An English Electric Canberra, a British first-generation jet-powered medium bomber flown by Squadron Leader A Callard, becomes the first jet to make an unrefuelled Transatlantic flight. Taking 4 hours 37 minutes it flew almost 1,800 nautical miles (3,300km) from RAF Aldergrove in Northern Ireland to Gander in Newfoundland. *Interesting facts: A total of 1347 Canberra's were produced and of the 925 built in the U.K. 773 were delivered to the RAF. Photo: Canberra WJ874 in 2005 painted to represent the first prototype flown in 1949.*

| 22nd | The 4th British Film and Television Awards (BAFTAS) take place at the Odeon Theatre in Leicester Square, London, to honour the best films of 1950; the BAFTA Award for Best Film is won by All About Eve, starring Bette Davis, Anne Baxter and George Sanders. |
| 22nd | The film noir Pool of London is released and becomes the first British film to portray an interracial relationship. |

MAR

12th March: The character Dennis the Menace first appears in The Beano comic (issue 452 cover dated the 17th March 1951). *Interesting facts: The creation of Dennis the Menace saw sales of The Beano soar. In September 1974 (issue 1678) he replaced Biffo the Bear on the front cover and has been there ever since. Pictured: The first ever appearance of Dennis the Menace in the Beano - he didn't put on his stripey jersey for another few weeks and wouldn't bump into his future best pal Gnasher until 1968.*

| 13th | Pineapple Poll, a Gilbert and Sullivan-inspired comic ballet created by choreographer John Cranko with arranger Sir Charles Mackerras, is premiered at Sadler's Wells Theatre by the Sadler's Wells Ballet. *Follow up: The ballet was a critical and popular success and today remains in the repertoire of the Birmingham Royal Ballet.* |
| 17th | Brian Statham makes his Test cricket debut against New Zealand at Christchurch. A right arm fast bowler who played for Lancashire County Cricket Club from 1950 to 1968, he would go on to compete for England in nine overseas tours and 70 Test Matches between 1951 and 1965. |

11th April: The Stone of Scone, the traditional coronation stone of Scottish monarchs, English monarchs and more recently British monarchs, resurfaces on the altar of Arbroath Abbey in Scotland after having been stolen from Westminster Abbey on Christmas Day 1950 by Scottish nationalists. *Photo: The Stone of Scone being recovered from Arbroath Abbey after being handed to the Custodian of the Abbey James Wiseheart by the Scottish Nationalists.*

17th	The British Amphion-class submarine HMS Affray sinks off Alderney in the English Channel killing all 75 crew members. *Follow up: A board of Inquiry failed to provide any satisfactory explanation as to why Affray was lost and questions still remain to this day. NB: Affray, built in the closing stages of the Second World War, was the last Royal Navy submarine to be lost at sea.*
17th	Seven dockers' leaders are acquitted at the Old Bailey after being charged with conspiracy to incite dockers to strike. They had been charged under a wartime regulation intended to prevent industrial disputes after the Transport and General Workers Union had accepted a wage offer less than the Dockers Charter demand.
17th	The Peak District National Park is established as the first national park in the United Kingdom. *Fun facts: Three other National Parks were established in 1951; The Lake District, Snowdonia and Dartmoor.*
19th	Miss Sweden, Kiki Haakonson, carries off the first Miss World title at the Lyceum Ballroom in London.
22nd	Korean War: Battle of the Imjin River: Over 3 days the 29th Infantry Brigade of the British Army (serving with the UN) put up brave but ultimately unsuccessful resistance to the Chinese advance despite facing a numerically superior enemy. The last stand of the 1st Battalion The Gloucestershire Regiment at Hill 235 has become an important part of British military history and tradition.
23rd	Aneurin Bevan, recently appointed as Minister of Labour and National Service, together with John Freeman and Harold Wilson, resign from the government in protest at Hugh Gaitskell's announcement in the Budget to introduce prescription charges for dental care and spectacles (in order to meet the financial demands imposed by the Korean War).

APR

| 28th | Newcastle United win the FA Cup for the fourth time with a 2-0 win over Blackpool at Wembley Stadium. |

MAY

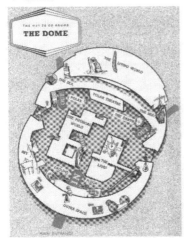

3rd May: George VI opens the Festival of Britain's centrepiece in London and people flock to the South Bank site to wander around the Dome of Discovery, gaze at the Skylon, and generally enjoy the festival of national celebration. *Festival information: Focusing entirely on Britain and its achievements, the Festival became a "beacon for change" that proved immensely popular. Events were held in every part of the U.K. with the South Bank Exhibition attracting some 8.5 million visitors, over half of them from outside London. NB: This was the last major public event attended by King George VI and Queen Elizabeth together before his death a year later.*

| 5th | The Ferranti NIMROD computer is presented at the Science Museum (London) during the Festival of Britain. It is designed exclusively to play Nim and is the first instance of a digital computer made specifically to play a game. |
| 28th | Spike Milligan's radio comedy programme Crazy People (subsequently renamed The Goon Show after the first series) premieres on the BBC. |

JUN

28th	The Ealing comedy film The Lavender Hill Mob premieres at the Marble Arch Odeon cinema in London. *Follow up: The film proved very popular at the British box office and went on to win the Academy Award for Best Writing, Story and Screenplay, and the BAFTA Award for Best British Film. Additionally, Alec Guinness, who played Henry "Dutch" Holland in the film, was nominated for the Academy Award of Best Actor in a Leading Role.*
29th	An explosion at the Easington Colliery in County Durham leaves 83 people dead (including 2 rescue workers).
29th	Treacherous British diplomats Guy Burgess and Donald Maclean, members of the Cambridge Five spy ring, defect to the Soviet Union.

JUL

2nd	Workington A.F.C. are elected to the Football League in place of New Brighton A.F.C. (they will compete in the Football League Third Division North for the 1951-52 season).

10th July: Boxer Randy Turpin beats the American Sugar Ray Robinson (considered by many to be the greatest boxer of all time) in front of a crowd of 18,000 at Earls Court in London to become world middleweight champion. *Fun facts: In winning the fight Turpin became the first British fighter to hold the world middleweight title since Bob Fitzsimmons in 1891. Robinson, who had been unbeaten as an amateur and had only lost one fight out of a total of 132 as a professional, regained his title just 64-days later in front of a crowd of 61,370 at the Polo Grounds in New York. Photo: Randolph Turpin (who was inducted into the International Boxing Hall of Fame in 2001) and his promoter Jack Solomons celebrating Turpin's win over Sugar Ray Robinson at Earl's Court.*

JUL

16th	Len Hutton, often described as one of the greatest batsmen in the history of cricket, scores his 100th 100 at The Oval.
17th	The Abbey Steelworks (now the Tata Steel Strip Products UK Port Talbot Works) opens at Margam in South Wales. *Fun facts: By the mid-1960s the steelworks at Port Talbot had grown to be the largest steel-producing complex in Europe, giving direct employment to over 18,000 men and women from south Wales.*
26th	Walt Disney's 13th animated feature film Alice in Wonderland premieres in London. *NB: Alice in Wonderland is regarded as one of Disney's greatest animated classics and notably one of the biggest cult classics in the animation medium.*

AUG

18th	Cricketer all-rounder Raymond Illingworth makes his first-class debut for Yorkshire. *Fun facts: In a career lasting 32 years he played for England in 61 Tests and 3 ODIs (1958-1973), with five seasons as their captain (1969-1973). During his time playing first-class cricket he notably took 2,000 wickets and made over 20,000 runs.*
26th	Vincente Minnelli's musical comedy film An American in Paris premieres in London. *NB: With music by George Gershwin and starring Gene Kelly and Leslie Caron, the film is an enormous success garnering eight Academy Award nominations and winning six (including Best Picture).*

SEP

10th	Britain begins an economic boycott of Iran after Iran nationalises the Anglo-Iranian Oil Company.
11th	American born Florence Chadwick becomes the first woman to swim English Channel in both directions after crossing from England to France in a time of 16 hours 22 minutes; she completed the France to England leg on the 9th August 1950 in a time of 13 hours 20 minutes.
14th	A rebuilt and extended Fawley Refinery is opened by Prime Minister Clement Attlee. Situated on Southampton Water it has an initial estimated capacity of 157,000 barrels (25,000m3) per day (around one third of U.K. demand at that time).
23rd	George VI has his left lung removed by pioneering Welsh thoracic surgeon Clement Price Thomas after a malignant tumour was found.
26th	The Rock and Ice Club is formed by a group of climbers in Manchester. *Note: Amongst these founders were Don Whillans and Joe Brown who were at the forefront of British climbing in the 1950s and 1960s.*
30th	The Festival of Britain ends.

OCT

6th	The Malayan High Commissioner Sir Henry Gurney is killed in an ambush by communist insurgents from the Malayan Communist Party; a chance killing, the guerrillas only learn that Gurney is amongst the dead from news reports.

15th | Exercise Surprise Packet, the largest British peacetime military exercise ever held in Britain, takes place over 8 counties of Southern England. Involving some 50,000 troops the manoeuvres last 4 days.

17th | The Austin A30 small family car is launched as the "New Austin Seven" at the Earls Court Motor Show. At launch the A30 cost £507 (equivalent to £16,045 in 2019), undercutting its competition the Morris Minor by £62.

26th October: General Election: After six years in power Clement Attlee's Labour government is defeated by Winston Churchill's Conservative Party (despite it winning the popular vote and achieving its highest-ever total vote). The election marks the return of Winston Churchill as Prime Minister and the beginning of the Labour Party's thirteen-year spell in opposition. *Photo: Winston Churchill and his wife Clementine at St Barnabus Secondary School in Woodford Green, Essex, as his constituency results are read out.*

31st | After isolated experiments the first Zebra crossings, with black and white stripes and Belisha beacons on either side of the road, are approved. Introduced because the number of deaths on the roads was increasing, the first Zebra crossing appears in Slough, Berkshire. *Fun facts: The globes on the Belisha beacons were originally made of glass but were replaced in 1952 with plastic because children kept throwing stones and smashing them.*

31st | Egypt unilaterally abrogates the Anglo-Egyptian treaty of 1936 which permitted Britain to keep troops in Egypt to protect the Suez Canal.

NOV

2nd | 6,000 British troops from the 1st Infantry Division are flown into Egypt to deal with anti-British disturbances at Fayid in the Canal Zone of Egypt; they will soon be joined by the Grenadier Guards and The Cameron Highlanders.

NOV

3rd — Express Dairies opens Britain's first supermarket under the Premier Supermarket brand in Streatham, South London (it was the first to qualify as a supermarket because it was self-service and had a floor space of more than 2,500sq ft.). The idea came from the chairman's son in law Patrick Galvani and was an instant success with 1,500 shoppers passing through its doors on the opening day. *Follow up: While the average U.K. store in 1951 was making £98 a week the Streatham outlet was soon raking in £1,000 every seven days. Within 14 years Express Dairies had opened 39 other stores and had been eagerly followed by other major competitors including Sainsbury's and Tesco.*

8th — The bank rate, maintained at 2% since the 26th October 1939, is raised to 2.5%.

17th — LEO becomes the world's first computer to run a full commercial business application, "Bakery Valuations". Constructed for the bakers J. Lyons and Co., LEO (Lyons Electronic Office) used 6,000 valves and took over a whole room.

20th — General Sir George Erskine orders the evacuation of several hundred British service families in Ismailia (in the Suez Canal Zone of Egypt) to be speeded up after weekend battles claim the lives of five British soldiers and nine Egyptian civilians.

22nd — Established by Dr John Berry in his role as Director of Nature Conservancy in Scotland, Beinn Eighe becomes Britain's first national nature reserve.

27th — The Prime Minister's Resignation Honours are announced in the London Gazette to mark the resignation of Prime Minister Clement Attlee. *NB: The London Gazette has published all Prime Minister's Resignation Honours lists since 1895.*

DEC

1st — Benjamin Britten's opera Billy Budd premieres at the Royal Opera House in Covent Garden. Performed in four acts and conducted by Britten himself, it receives 17 curtain calls.

10th — British physicists John Cockcroft and Ernest Walton jointly share the Nobel Prize in Physics "for their pioneer work on the transmutation of atomic nuclei by artificially accelerated atomic particles".

25th — King George VI makes his Christmas Speech to the Commonwealth (the speech was recorded in advance on account of his failing health).

31st — Prime Minister Winston Churchill and the Foreign Secretary Anthony Eden head off to America on the Queen Mary for talks with President Truman. *Follow up: Talks between Churchill and Truman saw an agreement to allow the U.S. to use British bases for "common defence" of the two countries.*

65 WORLDWIDE NEWS & EVENTS

1. 6th January: Ganghwa massacre: Over a period of 3 days hundreds of South Korean communist sympathisers are slaughtered by South Korean forces, South Korean Police forces and pro-South Korean militiamen.

2. 8th January: A cahow that had died flying into a lighthouse leads to the discovery of 18 further nesting pairs. This nocturnal ground-nesting seabird, otherwise known as the Bermuda petrel, was thought to have been extinct since 1615. *Fun fact: The cahow is the national bird of Bermuda.*

3. 8th January: The United Nations headquarters officially moves to the Secretariat Building in New York City.

4. 15th January: In a court in West Germany, Ilse Koch, the "Witch of Buchenwald" (wife of the commandant of the Buchenwald and Majdanek Nazi concentration camps), is sentenced to life imprisonment for her crimes.

5. 18th January: Mount Lamington, a stratovolcano in the Oro Province of Papua New Guinea, starts to erupt. *Follow up: Three days later there is a violent eruption and a large part of the northern side of the mountain is blown away. The pyroclastic flows and subsequent eruptions of dust and ash cause considerable damage and lead to the deaths of some 3,000 people; more than 5,000 people are made homeless.*

6. 19th January: A series of avalanches in the Swiss, Austrian and Italian Alps kill at least 126 people and injure hundreds of others.

7. 29th January: Eighteen-year-old Elizabeth Taylor gets divorced from hotel heir Conrad 'Nicky' Hilton Jr. just 205 days after saying "I do".

8. 1st February: The United Nations General Assembly condemns the People's Republic of China's aggression in the Korean War (Resolution 498). *NB: It is the first time the United Nations had treated a nation as an aggressor.*

9. 12th February: The Shah (Emperor) of Iran Mohammad Reza Pahlavi marries Soraya Esfandiary-Bakhtiari at the Marble Palace in Tehran. *Notes: Mohammad Reza Pahlavi was the last Shah of Iran and reigned from the 16th September 1941 until his overthrow in the Iranian Revolution on the 11th February 1979.*

10. 13th February: The largest and most widespread industrial dispute in New Zealand history begins as up to twenty thousand workers go on strike in support of waterfront workers protesting against financial hardships and poor working conditions. The dispute, sometimes referred to as the waterfront lockout or waterfront strike, lasts for 151 days (until the 15th July).

11. 19th February: Jean Lee becomes the last woman to be hanged in Australia when, along with her 2 pimps, she is executed for the murder and torture of William Kent, a 73-year-old bookmaker.

12. 28th February: The 8th Golden Globe Awards, honouring the best in film for 1950, are held at Ciro's nightclub in West Hollywood, California. The winners include Sunset Boulevard, Jose Ferrer and Gloria Swanson.

13. 3rd March: Jackie Brenston and his Delta Cats (the Delta Cats were actually Ike Turner's Kings of Rhythm) record Rocket 88 at Sam Phillips' Sun Studio in Memphis, Tennessee. *Fun facts: Rocket 88 reached No.1 on the U.S. Billboard R&B chart and many music writers acknowledge its importance in the development of rock and roll music, with several considering it to be the first rock and roll record.*

14.	7th March: Operation Ripper: In Korea United Nations troops, led by U.S. Eighth Army General Matthew Ridgway, begin an assault against the Chinese People's Volunteer Army (PVA) and Korean People's Army (KPA) around Seoul, Hongch'on and Chuncheon.
15.	14th March: Korean War: United Nations forces (including elements of the Republic of Korea Army (ROK) 1st Infantry Division and the U.S. 3rd Infantry Division) liberate Seoul.
16.	25th March: The 5th Annual Tony Awards are held at the Waldorf-Astoria Grand Ballroom in New York City. The winners include Guys and Dolls (best musical) and Rose Tattoo (best play).

17. 29th March: The 23rd Academy Awards Ceremony, awarding Oscars for the best in films for 1950, are held at RKO Pantages Theatre in Hollywood, California. Joseph L. Mankiewicz's drama film All About Eve (which received 14 Oscar nominations, beating the previous record of 13 set by Gone with the Wind at the 12th Academy Awards in 1940) wins the Best Motion Picture. The best Actor / Actress Awards go to José Ferrer (in Cyrano de Bergerac) and Judy Holliday (in Born Yesterday). *Photos: Presenter Gloria Swanson with José Ferrer and Judy Holliday / Director Joseph L. Mankiewicz.*

18.	29th March: The Rodgers and Hammerstein stage musical The King and I opens at Broadway's St. James Theatre. In a run lasting nearly three years the musical (specifically written for actress and veteran leading lady Gertrude Lawrence) also stars the young actor and television director Yul Brynner. *NB: The musical was an immediate hit and would go on to win Tony Awards for Best Musical, Best Actress (for Lawrence), and Best Featured Actor (for Brynner).*
19.	11th April: U.S. President Harry S. Truman relieves General Douglas MacArthur of his Far Eastern commands. *NB: MacArthur had made a number of public statements contradicting the Truman administration's policies.*
20.	12th April: The Israeli Knesset (the unicameral national legislature of Israel) passes a resolution establishing the 27th day of Nisan as Yom Hashoah (Holocaust Memorial Day).
21.	18th April: The Treaty of Paris (1951) is adopted establishing the European Coal and Steel Community (ECSC); it is signed by France, West Germany, Italy, Belgium, Luxembourg, and the Netherlands.

22.	20th April: As the 4th Cannes Film Festival comes to a close the "Grand Prix du Festival International du Film" is awarded to two films: Miss Julie, directed by Alf Sjoberg, and Miracle in Milan, directed by Vittorio De Sica.
23.	21st April: The National Olympic Committee of the Soviet Union is formed (it is recognised by International Olympic Committee on the 7th May 1951). *Interesting facts: The Soviet Union had not previously participated in international sporting events on ideological grounds however Soviet officials and leaders now believed it a useful method of promoting Communism. The USSR would go on to compete in their first Olympic Games at Helsinki, Finland, in 1952.*
24.	24th April: A train approaching Sakuragichō Station in Yokohama, Japan, hits a loose overhead wire causing a short circuit and starting a fire which kills 106 people and injures 92.
25.	28th April: The Australian federal election sees Robert Menzies' Liberal-Country Coalition re-elected to government after defeating the Labor Party led by former Prime Minister Ben Chifley.
26.	1st May: The Grand Théâtre de Genève opera house in Geneva, Switzerland, is almost destroyed in a fire.
27.	7th May: The Pulitzer Prize for Fiction is awarded to Conrad Richter for his novel The Town (the third instalment of his trilogy The Awakening Land).
28.	15th May: A military coup in Bolivia sees Hugo Ballivián (Commander of the Bolivian Armed Forces) overthrow President Mamerto Urriolagoitía.
29.	23rd May: The Tibetan government signs the Seventeen Point Agreement (for the Peaceful Liberation of Tibet) with the People's Republic of China.
30.	4th July: American Bell Labs research group manager William Shockley, and fellow physicists John Bardeen and Walter Brattain, announce the invention of the bipolar junction transistor at Murray Hill, New Jersey. *NB: The three scientists were jointly awarded the 1956 Nobel Prize in Physics for "their researches on semiconductors and their discovery of the transistor effect".*
31.	11th July: In the U.S. suburb of Cicero in Chicago, Illinois, a mob of 4,000 whites attack an apartment building that has been rented to African-American World War II veteran Harvey E. Clark Jr and his family. *Notes: The riot lasts several nights, causes $20,000 in damages, and receives worldwide condemnation.*
32.	11th July: West Germany joins UNESCO (the United Nations Educational, Scientific and Cultural Organization).
33.	14th July: At Santa Anita Park in Arcadia, California, thoroughbred racehorse Citation wins the Hollywood Gold Cup by 4 lengths to become the first American horse to win over $1 million.
34.	16th July: King Leopold III of Belgium abdicates in favour of his son Baudouin.
35.	16th July: J. D. Salinger's coming-of-age story The Catcher in the Rye is published by Little, Brown and Company in New York City. *Fun facts: Consistently listed as one of the best novels of the twentieth century around one million copies are sold each year (total book sales to date are over 65 million).*
36.	18th July: Thirty-seven-year-old Jersey Joe Walcott knocks out Ezzard Charles in the 7th round in Pittsburgh, Pennsylvania, to become the oldest fighter to win a world heavyweight title.
37.	20th July: King Abdullah I of Jordan is assassinated by Palestinian Mustafa Shukri Ashu from the Husseini clan while attending Friday prayers at Al-Aqsa Mosque in Jerusalem. He is succeeded by his son Talal bin Abdullah.
38.	28th July: Kiss Me, Kate closes on Broadway after 1077 performances. *Fun facts: The musical, which premiered in 1948, is Cole Porter's only show to run for more than 1,000 performances on Broadway. In 1949 it won the first ever Tony Award for Best Musical.*

39.	29th July: The 38th Tour de France is won by Hugo Koblet of Switzerland.
40.	30th July: David Lean's film adaptation of the Charles Dickens novel Oliver Twist (1948) is finally shown in the U.S. after 10 minutes of supposedly anti-Semitic references and closeups of Alec Guinness as Fagin are cut. It will not be shown uncut in the U.S. until 1970.

41. 7th August: A Viking rocket (Viking 7) launched from White Sands in New Mexico reaches an altitude of 136 miles to beat the old 114-mile V-2 record for a single-stage rocket. *Interesting facts: The Viking rocket series of sounding rockets were designed and built by the Glenn L. Martin Company (now Lockheed-Martin) under the direction of the U.S. Naval Research Laboratory (NRL). Twelve Viking rockets were flown between 1949 and 1955.*

42.	9th August: General Francisco Craveiro Lopes is appointed President of Portugal.
43.	22nd August: The Harlem Globetrotters play at Olympic Stadium in Berlin before 75,052 fans.
44.	1st September: The U.S., Australia and New Zealand all sign a mutual defence pact called the ANZUS Treaty to co-operate on military matters in the Pacific Ocean region. *NB: Today the treaty is taken to relate to conflicts worldwide. It provides that an armed attack on any of the three parties would be dangerous to the others, and that each should act to meet the common threat.*
45.	8th September: The Treaty of San Francisco is signed by 48 nations at the War Memorial Opera House in San Francisco. *Follow up: The treaty came into force on April 28, 1952, and officially ended the American-led Allied occupation of Japan.*
46.	18th September: Tennessee Williams's film adaptation of A Streetcar Named Desire premieres in Beverly Hills, California. *Fun facts: The film saw Marlon Brando's rise to prominence as a major Hollywood film star and gave him the first of four consecutive Academy Award nominations for Best Actor.*
47.	29th September: Emil Zatopek, nicknamed the Czech Locomotive, becomes the first athlete to run more than 20km in a one hour run (he also sets the 20km world record in the same race).
48.	3rd October - 8th October: Korean War: In the First Battle of Maryang-san United Nations forces (primarily Australian) drive back the Chinese.

49.	14th October: The governments of Costa Rica, El Salvador, Guatemala, Honduras and Nicaragua sign a treaty creating the Organization of Central American States, to promote regional cooperation and unity.
50.	15th October: The progestin norethisterone, significant in creation of the combined oral contraceptive pill, is synthesised by Carl Djerassi, Luis E. Miramontes and George Rosenkranz at Syntex in Mexico City.
51.	16th October: Prime Minister Liaquat Ali Khan of Pakistan is assassinated by a hired assassin, Said Babrak.
52.	16th October: Judy Garland begins her legendary concerts in New York's Palace Theatre on Broadway. The show, original scheduled for a 4-week run, is extended to 19 weeks and breaks all box office records.
53.	24th October: President Truman declares an official end to war with Germany. *NB: The state of war had not been lifted off of Germany directly after World War 2 in order to give a reason for the necessity of occupation troops in the country.*
54.	26th October: Future world heavyweight boxing champion Rocky Marciano defeats former champion Joe Louis by TKO in the 8th round at New York's Madison Square Garden. *Notes: The fight is Louis's last professional bout and he ends his career with a record of 66 wins (52 by knockout) and 3 losses. Louis notably made 25 defences of his heavyweight title between 1937 and 1948, and was a world champion for 11 years and 10 months.*
55.	28th October: Juan Manuel Fangio of Argentina takes the Formula 1 World Drivers Championship after his win at the Spanish Grand Prix in Barcelona. *NB: Fangio went on to win the Drivers' Championship again in 1954, 1955, 1956 and 1957.*

56. 31st October: President Truman and his wife Bess welcome 25-year-old Princess Elizabeth and husband Prince Philip on a two-day visit to Washington D.C. *Photo: President Truman and Princess Elizabeth in the presidential limousine following the reception ceremony at Washington National Airport.*

57.	11th November: Juan Domingo Perón is re-elected president of Argentina after gaining 62.5% of the vote.

58.	14th November: The river Po bursts its banks beginning 11 days of flooding in northern Italy. At its zenith the flood reaches the Polesine near the river's delta and submerges hundreds of hectares of agricultural land lying below sea level, killing 84 people and leaving 180,000 homeless.
59.	4th December: Mount Hibok-Hibok (also known as Catarman Volcano) erupts unleashing boiling lava, poisonous gases and landslides on Camiguin Island in the Philippines. The eruption destroys nearly 7.3 square miles of land and kills over 3,000 people.
60.	11th December: U.S. baseball legend Joe DiMaggio announces to the press his decision to retire from baseball. The New York Yankees outfielder ends his thirteen-year career after rejecting owner Dan Topping's $100,000 offer for him to continue playing.
61.	16th December: The Salar Jung Museum is opened to the public by the Prime Minister of India, Jawaharlal Nehru. *NB: One of the largest museums in the world it was endowed to the nation after the death of Salar Jung III.*
62.	17th December: A paper entitled "We Charge Genocide: The Crime of Government Against the Negro People", describing genocide by the U.S. government against African Americans, is delivered to the United Nations.
63.	20th December: Experimental Breeder Reactor I (EBR-1), one of the world's first nuclear power plants, starts generating electricity in the American city of Arco in Idaho. *Fun facts: It initially produced sufficient electricity to illuminate four 200-watt light bulbs and subsequently went on be able to generate sufficient electricity to power its building.*
64.	24th December: Libya declares its independence as the United Kingdom of Libya; Idris I is proclaimed King.
65.	31st December: The Marshall Plan (an American initiative passed in 1948 for foreign aid to Western Europe after the end of World War II) expires after distributing more than US$12 billion in aid.

BIRTHS

British Personalities

BORN IN 1951

Helen Worth
b. 7th January 1951

Actress best known for portraying Gail Platt
in the ITV soap opera Coronation Street.

Phil Collins
b. 30th January 1951

Drummer, singer, songwriter, multi-
instrumentalist, record producer and actor.

Ken Bruce
b. 2nd February 1951

Broadcaster best known for hosting his
long-running show on BBC Radio 2.

Kevin Keegan, OBE
b. 14th February 1951

Football player and manager who was
capped 63 times for England.

Jane Seymour, OBE
b. 15th February 1951

British-American actress.

Gordon Brown, HonFRSE
b. 20th February 1951

Former Prime Minister and leader of the
Labour Party (2007-2010).

Phil Neal
b. 20th February 1951

Footballer who was capped 50 times for
England.

Derek Randall
b. 24th February 1951

First-class cricketer who played for
Nottinghamshire and England.

Steve Harley
b. 27th February 1951

Singer and songwriter best known as the
frontman of the rock group Cockney Rebel.

Kenny Dalglish, MBE
b. 4th March 1951

Football player and manager who was
capped 102 times for Scotland.

Chris Rea
b. 4th March 1951

Rock and blues singer-songwriter and guitarist.

Paul Barber
b. 18th March 1951

Actor with a career spanning more than 30 years.

Peter Davison
b. 13th April 1951

Television, stage and radio actor.

Louise Jameson
b. 20th April 1951

Theatre and television actress.

Paul Carrack
b. 22nd April 1951

Singer, songwriter, composer and multi-instrumentalist.

Antony Worrall Thompson
b. 1st May 1951

Restaurateur, celebrity chef, television presenter and radio broadcaster.

Selina Scott
b. 13th May 1951

Journalist and television presenter.

John Conteh, MBE
b. 27th May 1951

Boxer who held the WBC light-heavyweight title from 1974 to 1978.

Bonnie Tyler
b. 8th June 1951

Singer known for her distinctive husky voice.

Paul Boateng
b. 14th June 1951

Labour Party politician who became the UK's first mixed-race Cabinet Minister.

Trevor Eve
b. 1st July 1951

Film and television actor.

Lorraine Chase
b. 16th July 1951

Actress and former model.

John Deacon

b. 19th August 1951

Musician best known for being the bass guitarist for the rock band Queen.

Rob Halford

b. 25th August 1951

Singer, songwriter and lead vocalist of heavy metal band Judas Priest.

David Coverdale

b. 22nd September 1951

Rock singer best known for his work with Whitesnake and Deep Purple.

Gordon Sumner

b. 22nd October 1951

Musician and actor better known as Sting.

Graham Price, MBE

b. 24th November 1951

Rugby union player who won 41 caps for Wales and 12 for the British Lions.

Bill Bryson, OBE, HonFRS

b. 8th December 1951

American-British author and journalist.

Notable British Deaths

2nd Jan	Edith Bessie New (b. 17th March 1877) - Suffragette. New and fellow suffragette Mary Leigh were the first to use vandalism as a tactic to further their cause and were both arrested in June 1908 for breaking windows at 10 Downing Street (they were subsequently sentenced to two months in prison at Holloway for their crime).
29th Jan	Evan John Roberts (b. 8th June 1878) - Evangelist who was a leading figure of the 1904-1905 Welsh Christian Revival.
27th Feb	Sir Percy Malcolm Stewart, 1st Baronet (b. 9th May 1872) - Industrialist and philanthropist who incorporated The London Brick Company in the 1920s (at the time it was reputed to be the largest brick making company in the United Kingdom).

6th March: Ivor Novello (b. David Ivor Davies; 15th January 1893) - Welsh composer and actor who became one of the most popular British entertainers of the first half of the 20th century. *NB. The Ivor Novello Awards, for songwriting and composing, are named after the entertainer. They have been presented annually in London by the British Academy of Songwriters, Composers and Authors (BASCA) since 1956, and over 1,000 statuettes have been awarded to date.*

13th Mar	James Ingall Wedgwood (b. 24th March 1883) - The first Presiding Bishop of the Liberal Catholic Church.
31st Mar	Ralph Forbes (b. 30th September 1904) - Film and stage actor in both the United Kingdom and the United States.
5th Apr	Edward Coke (b. 5th February 1879) - Character actor known professionally as Edward Rigby who had roles in more than 150 films between 1933 and 1951.
6th Apr	Robert Broom, FRS, FRSE (b. 30th November 1866) - Scottish South African doctor and palaeontologist.

14th April: Ernest Bevin (b. 9th March 1881) - Statesman, trade union leader and Labour politician. He co-founded and served as general secretary of the Transport and General Workers' Union (1922-1940), was the Minister of Labour in the war-time coalition government, and served as Foreign Secretary in the post-war Labour government (his tenure saw the end of the Mandate of Palestine and the creation of the State of Israel).

22nd Apr	Horace St. John Kelly Donisthorpe (b. 17th March 1870) - Eccentric myrmecologist and coleopterist.

24th Apr	Sir Joseph Maclay, 1st Baron Maclay, PC (b. 6th September 1857) - Scottish businessman and public servant.
6th Jun	Lionel Hallam Tennyson, 3rd Baron Tennyson (b. 7th November 1889) - First-class cricketer who captained Hampshire and England. *Note: He was the grandson of Poet Laureate Alfred, Lord Tennyson.*
11th Jun	Walter Carruthers Sellar (b. 27th December 1898) - Scottish humourist who wrote for Punch.

3rd July: Gwendoline Elizabeth Davies, CH (b. 11th February 1882) - Philanthropist and patron of the arts who, together with her sister Margaret, is recognised as the most influential collector of Impressionist and 20th century art in Wales. *Fun facts: Davies and her sister created one of the most important private collections of art in Britain and donated their total of 260 works to what is now the National Museum Wales.*

21st Aug	Leonard Constant Lambert (b. 23rd August 1905) - Composer, conductor and author.
9th Sep	Cecil William Turpie Gray (b. 19th May 1895) - Music critic, author and composer.
27th Sep	Sir Robert John Thomas, 1st Baronet (b. 23rd April 1873) - Welsh businessman and Liberal Party politician.
6th Oct	Sir Henry Lovell Goldsworthy Gurney, KCMG, KStJ (b. 27th June 1898) - Colonial administrator who served in various posts throughout the British Empire. *Note: He was assassinated by communist insurgents whilst serving as high commissioner in the Federation of Malaya.*
10th Dec	Algernon Henry Blackwood, CBE (b. 14th March 1869) - Broadcasting narrator, journalist, novelist and short story writer, and among the most prolific ghost story writers in the history of the genre.

15th December: James Eric Drummond, 7th Earl of Perth, GCMG, CB, PC, DL (b. 17th August 1876) - Politician and diplomat as well as the first Secretary-General of the League of Nations (1920-1933). After his time with the League of Nations he became British ambassador to Rome (1933-1939) and later, chief adviser on foreign publicity in the Ministry of Information (1939-1940). In 1946 he became deputy leader of the Liberal Party in the House of Lords.

POPULAR MUSIC

Jimmy Young	No.1	Too Young
Teresa Brewer	No.2	Longing For You
Les Paul & Mary Ford	No.3	Mockin' Bird Hill
Patti Page	No.4	Tennessee Waltz
Hoagy Carmichael	No.5	My Resistance is Low
Mel Blanc	No.6	I Taut I Taw A Puddy Tat
Nelson Eddy & Jo Stafford	No.7	With These Hands
Billy Cotton & His Band	No.8	The Petite Waltz
Teddy Johnson	No.9	Beloved, Be Faithful
Frankie Laine	No.10	Jezebel

NB. The first British record sales chart, The Hit Parade, did not appear until 14th November 1952. Prior to this popular songs were measured by sales of sheet music which was purchased both by professional musicians who performed live in pubs, clubs and theatres, and by keen amateurs. A song could often be perfomed by many different combinations of singers and bands, and the contemporary charts would list the song without clarifying whose version was the major hit. With this in mind it should be noted that although the above chart has been compiled with best intent it remains subjective.

Jimmy Young
Too Young

Label:	Written by:	Length:
Polygon	Lippmann / Dee	3 mins 22 secs

Sir Leslie Ronald Young, CBE (b. 21st September 1921 - d. 7th November 2016) was a singer, disc jockey and radio personality. He had two No.1 records early in his career (Unchained Melody and The Man from Laramie, both in 1955), as well as several other top ten hits, but became best known for his long-running show on BBC Radio 2. Young received an OBE in 1979, a CBE in 1993, and at the beginning of 2002 was knighted for services to broadcasting.

Teresa Brewer
Longing For You

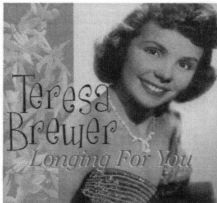   

Label:	Written by:	Length:
London Records	Władysław Daniłowski	2 mins 51 secs

Teresa Brewer (b. Theresa Veronica Breuer; 7th May 1931 - d. 17th October 2007) was a singer whose style incorporated country, jazz, R&B, musicals and novelty songs. She was one of the most prolific and popular female singers of the 1950s recording nearly 600 songs. Her 1950 No.1 hit Music, Music, Music went on to sell over a million copies and earned her the nickname Miss Music. Brewer has a star on the Hollywood Walk of Fame was inducted into the Hit Parade Hall of Fame in 2007.

3 Les Paul & Mary Ford
Mockin' Bird Hill

Label:	**Written by:**	**Length:**
Capitol Records	Ford / Horton	2 mins 16 secs

Les Paul (b. Lester William Polsfuss; 9th June 1915 - d. 12th August 2009) and **Mary Ford** (b. Iris Colleen Summers; 7th July 1924 - d. 30th September 1977) were a popular husband-and-wife musical duo who both sang and played guitars. Between 1950 and 1954 the couple had 16 top-ten hits in the United States, and in 1951 alone sold more than six million records. Paul was one of the pioneers of the solid-body electric guitar and his techniques served as inspiration for the Gibson Les Paul.

4 Patti Page
Tennessee Waltz

Label:	**Written by:**	**Length:**
Mercury	Pee Wee King / Redd Stewart	3 mins 3 secs

Patti Page (b. Clara Ann Fowler; 8th November 1927 - d. 1st January 2013) was a singer of pop and country music, and occasional actress. Page signed with Mercury Records in 1947 and became their first successful female artist. She was the top-charting female vocalist and best-selling female artist of the 1950s, and during her six-decade long career sold over 100 million records. Tennessee Waltz was Page's signature song and is recognised today as one of the official songs of the U.S. state of Tennessee.

Hoagy Carmichael
My Resistance is Low

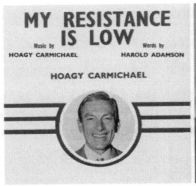  

Label:	Written by:	Length:
Brunswick	Adamson / Carmichael	2 mins 48 secs

Hoagland Howard 'Hoagy' Carmichael (b. 22nd November 1899 - d. 27th December 1981) was a singer, songwriter and actor. He was one of the most successful Tin Pan Alley songwriters of the 1930s and was among the first singer-songwriters in the age of mass media to utilise new communication technologies, such as television and the use of electronic microphones and sound recordings. Carmichael composed several hundred songs, including 50 that achieved hit record status.

Mel Blanc
I Taut I Taw A Puddy Tat

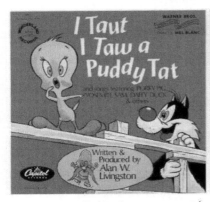  

Label:	Written by:	Length:
Capitol Records	Livingston / May / Foster	2 mins 53 secs

Melvin Jerome Blanc (b. 30th May 1908 - d. 10th July 1989) was a voice actor and radio personality. After beginning his over-60-year career performing in radio, he became known for his work in animation as the voices of Bugs Bunny, Daffy Duck, Porky Pig, and most of the other characters from the Looney Tunes and Merrie Melodies theatrical cartoons during the golden age of American animation. Blanc was nicknamed "The Man of a Thousand Voices" and is regarded today as one of the most influential people in the voice acting industry.

Nelson Eddy & Jo Stafford
With These Hands

Columbia Label:	Written by:	Length:
Brunswick	Silver / Davis	2 mins 45 secs

Nelson Ackerman Eddy (b. 29th June 1901 - d. 6th March 1967) was a singer, baritone and actor who appeared in 19 musical films during the 1930s and 1940s. He was one of the first "crossover" stars and was the highest paid singer in the world in his heyday. **Jo Elizabeth Stafford** (b. 12th November 1917 - d. 16th July 2008) was a traditional pop music singer and occasional actress whose career spanned five decades. Admired for the purity of her voice by 1955 she had achieved more worldwide record sales than any other female artist.

Billy Cotton & His Band
The Petite Waltz

Label:	Written by:	Length:
Decca	Heyne / Ellington / Claire	3 mins 4 secs

William Edward 'Billy' Cotton (b. 6th May 1899 - d. 25th March 1969) was a band leader, entertainer, accomplished racing driver and amateur footballer whose musical career began in the 1920s. One of the few whose orchestras survived the British dance band era, Cotton is now mainly remembered as a 1950s and 1960s radio and television personality (the BBC's Billy Cotton Band Show ran from 1949 to 1968 on radio, and from 1957 on television).

Teddy Johnson
Beloved, Be Faithful

Label:	Written by:	Length:
Columbia	Drake / Shirl	2 mins 58 secs

Edward Victor 'Teddy' Johnson (b. 4th September 1919 - d. 6th June 2018) was a singer, entertainer, drummer and disc jockey. Johnson is best remembered as part of the husband-and-wife duo 'Pearl and Teddy' with wife Pearl Lavinia Carr (b. 2nd November 1921 - d. 16th February 2020). Together they gained their highest profile during the 1950s and early 1960s, and notably came second in the 1960 Eurovision Song Contest in London with their song Sing, Little Birdie.

Frankie Laine
Jezebel

Label:	Written by:	Length:
Columbia	Wayne Shanklin	3 mins 7 secs

Frankie Laine (b. Francesco Paolo LoVecchio; 30th March 1913 - d. 6th February 2007) was a singer, songwriter and actor whose career spanned 75 years from his first concerts with a marathon dance company in 1930, to his final performance in 2005 with the song That's My Desire. Laine was one of the most popular vocalists of the 1950s and during his career sold over 100 million records. In recognition of his contributions to the music and television industry he has two stars on the Hollywood Walk of Fame and has been inducted into the Hit Parade Hall of Fame.

1951: TOP FILMS

1. **An American In Paris** - *MGM*
2. **A Streetcar Named Desire** - *Warner Bros.*
3. **A Place In The Sun** - *Paramount Pictures*
4. **Quo Vadis** - *MGM*
5. **The African Queen** - *United Artists*

OSCARS

Best Picture: An American In Paris
Most Nominations: A Streetcar Named Desire (12)
Most Wins: An American In Paris / A Place In The Sun (6)

Best Director: George Stevens - *A Place In The Sun*

Best Actor: Humphrey Bogart - *The African Queen*
Best Actress: Vivien Leigh - *A Streetcar Named Desire*
Best Supporting Actor: Karl Malden - *A Streetcar Named Desire*
Best Supporting Actress: Kim Hunter - *A Streetcar Named Desire*

The 24th Academy Awards, honouring the best in film for 1951, were presented on the 20th March 1952 at RKO Pantages Theatre in Hollywood, California.

AN AMERICAN IN PARIS

Directed by: Vincente Minnelli - Runtime: 1h 54min

Three friends struggle to find work in Paris and things become more complicated when two of them fall in love with the same woman.

Starring

Gene Kelly
b. 23rd August 1912
d. 2nd February 1996
Character:
Jerry Mulligan

Leslie Caron
b. 1st July 1931
Character:
Lise Bouvier

Oscar Levant
b. 27th December 1906
d. 14th August 1972
Character:
Adam Cook

Trivia

Goof When Jerry is painting Lise's portrait she poses with a red carnation in her hand. When they lean in to embrace the carnation falls on the ground and is momentarily out of view. When he bends down to pick it up it has magically transformed in to a red rose.

Interesting Facts Even though Vincente Minnelli is credited as the sole director he was sometimes tied up (with his divorce from Judy Garland and other directing projects) leaving Gene Kelly to take over.

The 17-minute dance sequence at the end of the picture took a month to film and cost $500,000.

Leslie Caron had suffered from malnutrition during WWII and was not used to the rigorous schedule of filming. Because of this she would tire easily and was only able to work every other day.

Oscar Levant, more of a pianist than an actor, signed onto the film because he was actually a friend of George Gershwin.

No words are spoken during the last 20 minutes and 25 seconds of the film.

Quotes **Jerry Mulligan:** That's... quite a dress you almost have on.
Milo Roberts: Thanks.
Jerry Mulligan: What holds it up?
Milo Roberts: Modesty.

Jerry Mulligan: Back home everyone said I didn't have any talent. They might be saying the same thing over here but it sounds better in French.

A Streetcar Named Desire

Directed by: Elia Kazan - Runtime: 2h 2min

Disturbed Blanche DuBois moves in with her sister in New Orleans and is tormented by her brutish brother-in-law while her reality crumbles around her.

Starring

Vivien Leigh
b. 5th November 1913
d. 8th July 1967
Character:
Blanche

Marlon Brando
b. 3rd April 1924
d. 1st July 2004
Character:
Stanley

Kim Hunter
b. 12th November 1922
d. 11th September 2002
Character:
Stella

Trivia

Goof | When Stanley is about to give Blanche the birthday "gift" of a ticket back home Marlon Brando opens the wallet to discover that the envelope with the ticket in it is missing. There is a sharp edit and the scene continues with the wallet missing from Stanley's hand, replaced with the envelope containing the ticket.

Interesting Facts | As the film progresses the set of the Kowalski apartment actually gets smaller to heighten the suggestion of Blanche's increasing claustrophobia.

Vivien Leigh, who suffered from bipolar disorder in real life, later had difficulties in distinguishing her real life from that of Blanche DuBois.

Marlon Brando was paid a sizeable $75,000 for his role in the film. This was partially due to an insider scoop that hailed Brando's acting style as the most revolutionary thing to hit Hollywood since the Talkies.

When the film was previewed in Santa Barbara in 1951 the director Elia Kazan's date was a then obscure contract starlet called Marilyn Monroe. *Note: It was Kazan who introduced her to her future husband Arthur Miller.*

The film is one of only two in history to win three Academy awards for acting.

Quotes | **Stanley Kowalski:** Man, liquor goes fast in the hot weather. You want a shot?
Blanche DuBois: No, I rarely touch it.
Stanley Kowalski: Well, there's some people that rarely touch it, but it touches them often.

Blanche DuBois: Whoever you are, I have always depended on the kindness of strangers.

Directed by: George Stevens - Runtime: 2h 2min

A poor boy gets a job working for his rich uncle and ends up falling in love with two women.

Starring

Montgomery Clift
b. 17th October 1920
d. 23rd July 1966
Character:
George Eastman

Elizabeth Taylor
b. 27th February 1932
d. 23rd March 2011
Character:
Angela Vickers

Shelley Winters
b. 18th August 1920
d. 14th January 2006
Character:
Alice Tripp

Trivia

Goof	When Alice Tripp is on her way home from the movie with George Eastman her brown and white shoes turn to black as she rounds the corner. *NB. When actress Shelley Winters pointed this out to director George Stevens he refused to reshoot the scene stating "If they're looking at her feet I can go home."*
Interesting Facts	Elizabeth Taylor's and Montgomery Clift's beach idyll was actually filmed in October at Lake Tahoe in California. Crew members had to hose snow off the ground and tree branches prior to filming. In the scene where Montgomery Clift and Dame Elizabeth Taylor are gaily zooming around the lake in a speedboat, Producer and Director George Stevens wanted the engine to sound more ominous so recordings of German Stuka dive bombers were used. The painstaking methods of George Stevens resulted in a final budget of $2,300,000 ($500,000 over budget) and more than four hundred thousand feet of film to edit. Stevens and Editor William Hornbeck worked on cutting the footage for more than a year. Anne Revere, who played Montgomery Clift's mother, became a victim of the McCarthy-era "Red Scare" blacklisting. After this film she didn't appear in another until 1970.
Quotes	**Angela:** Men are so disgustingly prompt. I think they do it just to put us women in a bad light. **Angela:** I'll love you for as long as I live. **George Eastman:** Love me for as long as I have left. Then forget me.

QUO VADIS

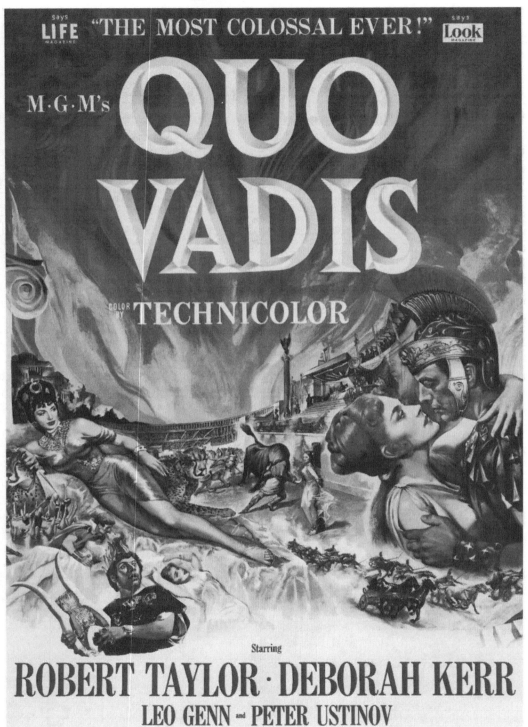

Directed by: Mervyn LeRoy - Runtime: 2h 46min

Fierce Roman commander Marcus Vinicius becomes infatuated with beautiful Christian hostage Lygia and begins questioning the tyrannical leadership of the despot Emperor Nero.

Starring

Robert Taylor
b. 5th August 1911
d. 8th June 1969
Character:
Marcus Vinicius

Deborah Kerr
b. 30th September 1921
d. 16th October 2007
Character:
Lygia

Leo Genn
b. 9th August 1905
d. 26th January 1978
Character:
Petronius

Trivia

Factual Error	The Colosseum, where the climax takes place, was actually built after Nero's death. *Note: It was one of Nero's successors, Vespasian, who razed Nero's palace in order to build the Colosseum.*
Interesting Facts	In his memoirs, "Dear Me" (1981), Sir Peter Ustinov recalled that MGM had sought him for the role of Emperor Nero but dithered for months refusing to commit. During this time he received numerous telegrams from the studio, one of which stated that they were concerned that he might be too young to play the notorious Roman Emperor. Ustinov replied that Emperor Nero died when he was thirty and that if they waited much longer he'd be too old. The studio cabled back: "Historical research has proved you correct. You have the part." Coincidentally Peter Ustinov was thirty-years-old when this movie was released.
	Clark Gable turned down the role of Marcus Vinicius because he thought the costume would make him look ridiculous.
	A young Sophia Loren has an uncredited (but easily spotted) bit part as a slave girl who strews flower petals in the path of Marcus Vinicius' chariot during the triumphal march.
	The film's huge box-office success was credited with saving MGM from bankruptcy.
Quote	**Vinicius:** *[speaking of Nero]* His new wife, Poppaea, sounds interesting - a harlot for an empress? **Petronius:** My dear Marcus, what a proletarian observation! You must know that a woman has no past when she mates with a god.

Directed by: John Huston - Runtime: 1h 45min

In WWI Africa a gin-swilling riverboat captain is persuaded by a strait-laced missionary to use his boat to attack an enemy warship.

Starring

Humphrey Bogart
b. 25th December 1899
d. 14th January 1957
Character:
Charlie Allnutt

Katharine Hepburn
b. 12th May 1907
d. 29th June 2003
Character:
Rose Sayer

Robert Morley
b. 26th May 1908
d. 3rd June 1992
Character:
Rev. Samuel Sayer

Trivia

Goofs	When Allnut goes underwater to check the propeller, the water lifts up the back of Humphrey Bogart's toupée revealing his bald head.
	In some close-ups of the African Queen her name is painted in white letters, other shots show the name of the boat in black lettering.
Interesting Facts	Sources claimed that everyone in the cast and crew got sick except Humphrey Bogart and John Huston who were purported to have avoided illness by essentially living on imported Scotch whiskey. Bogart later said, "All I ate was baked beans, canned asparagus and Scotch whiskey. Whenever a fly bit Huston or me it dropped dead."
	The African Queen was actually the L.S. Livingston which had been a working diesel boat for 40 years; the steam engine was a prop and the real diesel engine was hidden under stacked crates of gin and other cargo.
	Humphrey Bogart's Academy Award for Best Actor made him the last man born in the 19th century to win a leading role Oscar.
	Walt Disney used this film as the basis for Disneyland's Jungle Cruise attraction.
Quotes	**Charlie Allnut:** What are you being so mean for, Miss? A man takes a drop too much once in a while, it's only human nature. **Rose Sayer:** Nature, Mr. Allnut, is what we are put in this world to rise above.
	Captain of Louisa: By the authority vested in me by Kaiser William the Second I pronounce you man and wife. Proceed with the execution.

SPORTING WINNERS

FIVE NATIONS RUGBY

IRELAND

Position	Nation	Played	Won	Draw	Lost	For	Against	+/-	Points
1	**Ireland**	**4**	**3**	**1**	**0**	**21**	**16**	**+5**	**7**
2	France	4	3	0	1	41	27	+14	6
3	Wales	4	1	1	2	29	35	-6	3
4	Scotland	4	1	0	3	39	25	+14	2
5	England	4	1	0	3	13	40	-27	2

The 1951 and twenty-second series of the rugby union Five Nations Championship saw ten matches played between the 13th January and the 7th April. Including the previous incarnations as the Home Nations and Five Nations, this was the fifty-seventh series of the northern hemisphere rugby union championship. The competition saw Ireland win their 7th title but miss out on a second Grand Slam after drawing to Wales at Cardiff Arms Park.

Date	Team	Score	Team	Location
13-01-1951	France	14-12	Scotland	Paris
20-01-1951	Wales	23-5	England	Swansea
27-01-1951	Ireland	9-8	France	Dublin
03-02-1951	Scotland	19-0	Wales	Edinburgh
10-02-1951	Ireland	3-0	England	Dublin
24-02-1951	England	3-11	France	London
24-02-1951	Scotland	5-6	Ireland	Edinburgh
10-03-1951	Wales	3-3	Ireland	Cardiff
17-03-1951	England	5-3	Scotland	London
07-04-1951	France	8-3	Wales	Paris

CALCUTTA CUP

ENGLAND 5-3 SCOTLAND

The Calcutta Cup was first awarded in 1879 and is the rugby union trophy awarded to the winner of the match (currently played as part of the Six Nations Championship) between England and Scotland. The Cup was presented to the Rugby Football Union after the Calcutta Football Club in India disbanded in 1878; it is made from melted down silver rupees withdrawn from the club's funds.

BRITISH GRAND PRIX

José Froilán González in his race winning Ferrari at the 1951 British Grand Prix.

The 1951 British Grand Prix was held at Silverstone on the 14th July and was won by José Froilán González (from pole) over 90 laps of the 2.89-mile circuit. The race was not only González's first ever Formula 1 victory but also the first for the Scuderia Ferrari team.

Pos.	Country	Driver	Car
1	**Argentina**	**José Froilán González**	**Ferrari**
2	Argentina	Juan Manuel Fangio	Alfa Romeo
3	Italy	Luigi Villoresi	Ferrari

Silverstone first hosted the British Grand Prix in 1948 and is built on the site of the World War II Royal Air Force bomber station, RAF Silverstone. The airfield's three runways, in a classic WWII triangular format, lie within the outline of the present track.

1951 GRAND PRIX SEASON

Date	Race	Circuit	Winning Driver	Constructor
27-05	Swiss GP	Bremgarten	Juan Manuel Fangio	Alfa Romeo
30-05	Indy 500	Indianapolis	Lee Wallard	Kurtis Kraft-Offenhauser
17-06	Belgian GP	Spa	Giuseppe Farina	Alfa Romeo
01-07	French GP	Reims-Gueux	Fangio / Fagioli	Alfa Romeo
14-07	British GP	Silverstone	José Froilán González	Ferrari
29-07	German GP	Nürburgring	Alberto Ascari	Ferrari
16-09	Italian GP	Monza	Alberto Ascari	Ferrari
28-10	Spanish GP	Pedralbes	Juan Manuel Fangio	Alfa Romeo

The 1951 Formula One season was the fifth season of FIA Formula One motor racing. Juan Manuel Fangio won the championship with 31 points from Alberto Ascari (25 points) and José Froilán González (24 points).

GRAND NATIONAL - NICKEL COIN

The 1951 Grand National was the 105th renewal of this world famous horse race and took place at Aintree Racecourse near Liverpool on the 7th April. The winning horse was Nickel Coin who was trained by Jack O'Donoghue and ridden by jockey Johnny Bullock. An unprecedented twelve horses went at the first fence (either falling or being bought down). Of the 36 runners only three actually completed the course - all of the horses returned safely to the stables. *Photo: Nickel Coin taking the final fence at Aintree before going on to win the 1951 Grand National.*

	Horse	Jockey	Age	Weight	Odds
1st	**Nickel Coin**	**Johnny Bullock**	**9**	**10st-1lb**	**40/1**
2nd	Royal Tan	Phonsie O'Brien	7	10st-13lb	40/1
3rd	Derrinstown	Alan Power	11	10st-0lb	66/1

EPSOM DERBY - ARCTIC PRINCE

The Derby Stakes is Britain's richest horse race and the most prestigious of the country's five Classics. First run in 1780 this Group 1 flat horse race is open to 3-year-old thoroughbred colts and fillies. The race takes place at Epsom Downs in Surrey over a distance of one mile, four furlongs and 10 yards (2,423 metres) and is scheduled for early June each year. The 1951 Derby was won by Arctic Prince and ridden by jockey Chuck Spares.

Photo: Irish-bred Thoroughbred racehorse Arctic Prince (1948-1969) who was owned by Joseph McGrath and trained by Willie Stephenson.

FOOTBALL LEAGUE CHAMPIONS

England

Pos.	Team	W	D	L	F	A	Pts.
1	**Tottenham Hotspur**	**25**	**10**	**7**	**82**	**44**	**60**
2	Manchester United	24	8	10	74	40	56
3	Blackpool	20	10	12	79	53	50
4	Newcastle United	18	13	11	62	53	49
5	Arsenal	19	9	14	73	56	47

Scotland

Pos.	Team	W	D	L	F	A	Pts.
1	**Hibernian**	**22**	**4**	**4**	**78**	**26**	**48**
2	Rangers	17	4	9	64	37	38
3	Dundee	15	8	7	47	30	38
4	Heart of Midlothian	16	5	9	72	45	37
5	Aberdeen	15	5	10	61	50	35

FA CUP WINNERS - NEWCASTLE UNITED

Newcastle United   2-0   Blackpool

The 1951 FA Cup Final took place on the 28th April at Wembley Stadium in front of 100,000 fans. Newcastle United won the match to take the Cup for the fourth time; both goals were scored by Jackie Milburn. *Photo: Newcastle United's captain Joe Harvey is held aloft after their victory over Blackpool in the FA Cup final.*

SNOOKER - FRED DAVIS

Fred Davis 58-39 Walter Donaldson

The 1951 World Snooker Championship was held at the Tower Circus in Blackpool between the 30th October 1950 and 24th February 1951. For the fifth consecutive year the final was contested by Fred Davis and Walter Donaldson. Davis won his third World title defeating Donaldson 58-39 in the final. *Photo: Fred Davis (left) and Walter Donaldson in the 1948 Snooker World Championship final.*

GOLF - OPEN CHAMPIONSHIP - MAX FAULKNER

The 1951 Open Championship was the 80th to be played and was held between the 4th and 6th July at Royal Portrush Golf Club in County Antrim, Northern Ireland. Max Faulkner won his only major title and £300, two strokes ahead of runner-up Antonio Cerdá. Two-time defending champion Bobby Locke finished eight strokes back in a tie for sixth.

WIMBLEDON

Men's Singles Champion - Dick Savitt - United States
Ladies Singles Champion - Doris Hart - United States

The 1951 Wimbledon Championships was the 65th staging of tournament and took place on the outdoor grass courts at the All England Lawn Tennis and Croquet Club in Wimbledon, London. It ran from the 25th June until the 7th July and was the third Grand Slam tennis event of 1951.

Men's Singles Final:

Country	Player	Set 1	Set 2	Set 3
United States	Dick Savitt	6	6	6
Australia	Ken McGregor	4	4	4

Women's Singles Final:

Country	Player	Set 1	Set 2
United States	Doris Hart	6	6
United States	Shirley Fry	1	0

Men's Doubles Final:

Country	Players	Set 1	Set 2	Set 3	Set 4	Set 5
Australia	Ken McGregor / Frank Sedgman	3	6	6	3	6
Egypt / S.Africa	Jaroslav Drobný / Eric Sturgess	6	2	3	6	3

Women's Doubles Final:

Country	Players	Set 1	Set 2
United States	Shirley Fry / Doris Hart	6	13
United States	Louise Brough / Margaret duPont	3	11

Mixed Doubles Final:

Country	Players	Set 1	Set 2
Australia / United States	Frank Sedgman / Doris Hart	7	6
Australia	Mervyn Rose / Nancye Bolton	5	2

COUNTY CHAMPIONSHIP CRICKET - WARWICKSHIRE

1951 saw the fifty-second officially organised running of the County Championship. It ran from the 5th May to the 4th September and produced a surprise title for Warwickshire, their first for forty years and only the second in their history.

Pos.	Team	Pld.	W	L	LWF	DWF	DTF	DLF	ND	Pts.
1	**Warwickshire**	**28**	**16**	**2**	**0**	**6**	**0**	**4**	**0**	**216**
2	Yorkshire	28	12	3	0	10	0	1	2	184
3	Lancashire	28	8	1	1	9	0	5	4	136
4	Worcestershire	28	9	5	2	4	0	6	2	132
5	Glamorgan	28	8	3	1	7	0	6	3	128

ENGLAND VS SOUTH AFRICA - TEST SERIES

1st Test | Trent Bridge, 7th - 12th June - Result: South Africa win by 71 runs

Innings	Team	Score	Overs	Team	Score	Overs
1st Innings	South Africa	483/9d	240	England	419/9d	163.2
2nd Innings	South Africa	121	51.4	England	114	65.2

2nd Test | Lord's, 21st - 23rd June - Result: England win by 10 wickets

Innings	Team	Score	Overs	Team	Score	Overs
1st Innings	England	311	107.4	South Africa	115	64.5
2nd Innings	England	16/0	3.5	South Africa	211 (f/o)	96.2

3rd Test | Old Trafford, 5th - 10th July - Result: England win by 9 wickets

Innings	Team	Score	Overs	Team	Score	Overs
1st Innings	South Africa	158	84.3	England	211	85.3
2nd Innings	South Africa	191	78.2	England	142/1	51.3

4th Test | Headingley, 26th - 31st July - Result: Match drawn

Innings	Team	Score	Overs	Team	Score	Overs
1st Innings	South Africa	538	235.3	England	505	224.5
2nd Innings	South Africa	87/0	49	England		

5th Test | The Oval, 16th - 18th August - Result: England win by 4 wickets

Innings	Team	Score	Overs	Team	Score	Overs
1st Innings	South Africa	202	106.3	England	194	87
2nd Innings	South Africa	154	75.5	England	164/6	62.1

THE COST OF LIVING

EXQUISITE
Gaily coloured members of the *Nymphalidæ* family of South American butterflies clustered on the flowers of a Giant Saguaro cactus.

IMPERIAL ✠ LEATHER
The Toilet Luxuries of Exquisite Character

Cussons

COMPARISON CHART

	1951	1951 (+ Inflation)	2020	% Change
3 Bedroom House	£2,5000	£86,454	£234,853	+171.7%
Weekly Income	£4.19s.8d	£172.33	£619	+259.2%
Pint Of Beer	10d	£1.44	£3.79	+163.2%
Cheese (lb)	2s.3d	£3.89	£2.98	-23.4%
Bacon (lb)	2s.5d	£4.18	£2.94	-29.7%
The Beano	2d	29p	£2.75	+848.3%

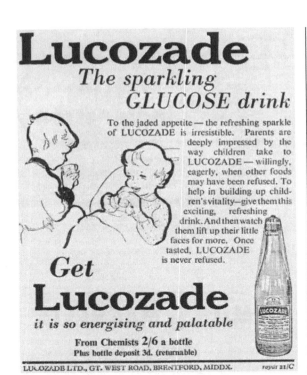

Lucozade

The sparkling GLUCOSE drink

To the jaded appetite — the refreshing sparkle of LUCOZADE is irresistible. Parents are deeply impressed by the way children take to LUCOZADE — willingly, eagerly, when other foods may have been refused. To help in building up children's vitality—give them this exciting, refreshing drink. And then watch them lift up their little faces for more. Once tasted, LUCOZADE is never refused.

Get Lucozade

it is so energising and palatable

From Chemists 2/6 a bottle
Plus bottle deposit 3d. (returnable)

LUCOZADE LTD., GT. WEST ROAD, BRENTFORD, MIDDX.   *royat 21/C*

Thanks to...

1865–1951

The family will appreciate that little addition of LEMCO BEEF EXTRACT. It makes all the difference to your cooking.

LEMCO THE ORIGINAL

Concentrated Beef Extract

AN OXO LIMITED PRODUCT

HOT DAY
FOR WALKING, SIR
says OLD HETHERS

It's that last hundred yards climb that does it, Sir, just when you think you're here. But I've got the cure for that thirst — Robinson's Barley Water. Its cool smoothness is so refreshing, a regular tonic as well as a drink.

Robinson's
Lemon or Orange
BARLEY WATER

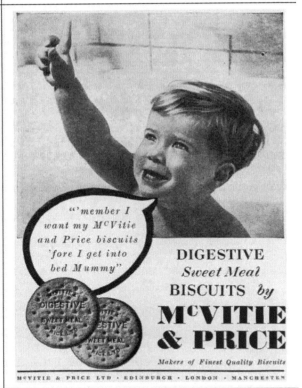

"'member I want my McVitie and Price biscuits 'fore I get into bed Mummy"

DIGESTIVE
Sweet Meal
BISCUITS *by*

McVITIE & PRICE

Makers of Finest Quality Biscuits

McVITIE & PRICE LTD · EDINBURGH · LONDON · MANCHESTER

COOPER'S *Household* AEROSOL

* 9 times more powerful than standard flysprays.

COOPER, McDOUGALL & ROBERTSON, LTD., BERKHAMSTED, HERTS.
IC/16

SHOPPING

Bread Loaf	6d
Welgar Shredded Wheat (large pkg.)	11½d
Fry's Milk Punch	4½d
Idris Soft Drink	3s
Carter's Quosh Fruit Squash	2s.9d
Lucozade	2s.6d
Brylfoam Cream Shampoo (tube)	9½d
Vaseline Liquid Shampoo	1s.6d
Odo-Ro-No Deodorant Cream	1s.6d
Phillips' Dental Magnesia Toothpaste	1s.4d
Chen Yu Lipstick	9s.6d
Chen Yu Nail Lacquer	7s.6d
Valderma Spot Cream (tube)	1s.8d
Optrex Eye Lotion	2s.6d
Milk Of Magnesia Tablets (30)	1s.3d
Crookes Halibut Oil Capsules (25)	2s.6d
Lixen Laxative Lozenges (bottle)	2s.6d
Dip Permanent Starcher (bottle)	1s.6d
Zoflora Perfumed Disinfectant	2s
Stergene Washing Cleaner	1s.9d

CLOTHES

Women's Clothing

Leslie Marshall & Co. Corduroy Jacket	£5.15s
Barrie & Co. Raincoat	£6.17s.6d
Bonnyclad Felt Beret	14s.6d
Anglo-American Fashions Rayon Jump Suit	£2
Dalena Models Floral Print Dress	19s.11d
Paris Vogue Sweater	8s.9d
Ronsol Polka Dot Styled Blouse	13s.6d
Barrie & Co. Gaberdine Skirt	12s.6d
Superfit Maternity Skirt	£1.5s
Kayser Bondor Brassiere	11s.9d
Brevitts Pageant Bouncer Shoes	£3.19s
P. Davis Leather Shoes	£1.2s.6d

Men's Clothing

Silk Lined Sports Coat	£5.7s
Ex-Transport Navy Blue Jacket	£1.3s.6d
Craig's Of London Cotton Shirt	7s.6d
Harringtons American Style Sports Shirt	18s.6d
Leda Elastic Waist Khaki Shorts	7s.6d
John White Oxford Style Shoes	£1.19s.6d
P. Davis Brown Leather Sandals	17s.11d

DEAUVILLE

"La Plage Fleurie"

SEASON : MAY TO OCTOBER
REGULAR AIR SERVICES
LONDON—DEAUVILLE
SPECIAL RETURN FARE £11

JUNE : WEEK-END SERVICES

JULY : DAILY SERVICES · AUGUST : TWICE DAILY SERVICES

JUNE : NORMANDY'S LOVELIEST MONTH
ALL SPORTS, Week-end Galas at the Ambassadeurs.

JULY : THE GREAT SPORTING MONTH.
Royal Aero Club Rally · International Horse Show.
Bridge, Fencing and Tennis Tournaments.
Races at Clairefontaine · Regattas.

NEW GOLF (2 courses) · International Seniors
Franco—British Parliamentary Matches.
(Tennis and Golf)

27-29 : Deauville Mixed Foursomes
(Coupe Thion de la Chaume)

NORMANDY HOTEL · ROYAL HOTEL · HOTEL DU GOLF

OTHER PRICES

Humber Hawk Car	£1035
Morris Minor Car	£520
Petrol (gallon)	3s.6d
Batley Concrete Garage	£50
Squires Gate Holiday Camp Blackpool (week)	£5.5s
Cinema Ticket	2d
NHS Glasses	23s - 35s
NHS False Teeth	£4.10s
Lectron Hearing Aids	19gns
Raymond Model F55 Radio	£19.0s.6d
Instrument Co. 4 Valve Mains Radio	£1.17s.6d
Penetray Infra-Red Health Lamp	£2.10s
Woodhouse Walnut Bedroom Suite	40gns
Ariel Mattress & Base	£70
J. Bull Portable Sewing Machine	£4.11s.8d
Smiths Mardale Presentation Clock	£4.5s
Macallen & Co. Festival Of Britain Clock	£1.4s
Ross Steptron Binoculars	£29
Gold Rotary Cocktail Watch	£15.18s.6d
Silver Mist Garden Shed	£8.2s.6d
Royal Enfield Motor Lawn Mower	£45.5s
Qualcast Mower	£7.2s.6d
Government Surplus Hosepipe (22-24ft long)	5s
Childs Turbo Metal Tricycle	19s.6d
Childs Musical Chair	£2.12s.6d
Gordons Gin	£1.13s.9d
Whiteway's Devon Cyder	1s.6d
Abdulla Virginia No.7 Cigarettes (20)	3s.10d
Woman's Weekly Magazine	3d

MONEY CONVERSION TABLE

Pounds / Shillings / Pence 1951 'Old Money'		Decimal Value	Value 2020 (Rounded)
Farthing	¼d	0.1p	4p
Half Penny	½d	0.21p	7p
Penny	1d	0.42p	14p
Threepence	3d	1.25p	43p
Sixpence	6d	2.5p	86p
Shilling	1s	5p	£1.73
Florin	2s	10p	£3.46
Half Crown	2s.6d	12.5p	£4.32
Crown	5s	25p	£8.65
Ten Shillings	10s	50p	£17.29
Pound	20s	£1	£34.58
Guinea	21s	£1.05	£36.31
Five Pounds	£5	£5	£172.91
Ten Pounds	£10	£10	£345.81

THE DAILY ROUND
THE COMMON TASK
IS MADE EASIER WITH THE FAMOUS

Swallow
Gadabout

The ideal machine for town and country homes . . . that odd shopping run . . . the casual call . . . home to business and an equally speedy return . . . in fact for all the little trips that make the daily round. Easy to handle and giving approximately 95 miles per gallon the Gadabout is equipped with the Villiers 10D. 122 c.c. two-stroke engine, 3-speed gear box with foot change, has a cruising speed of 30 m.p.h., comfortable seating and maximum weather protection. Obtainable from all authorised Swallow dealers.

SWALLOW COACHBUILDING CO (1935) LTD · THE AIRPORT · WALSALL · STAFFS

Printed in Great Britain
by Amazon